HEREDITY
AND GENETICS

UNDERSTANDING
MICROBES

Donna M. Bozzone, PhD

Enslow Publishing
101 W. 23rd Street
Suite 240
New York, NY 10011
USA

enslow.com

Published in 2019 by Enslow Publishing, LLC
101 W. 23rd Street, Suite 240, New York, NY 10011

Library of Congress Cataloging-in-Publication Data

Names: Bozzone, Donna M., author.
Title: Understanding microbes / Donna M. Bozzone, PhD.
Description: New York, NY : Enslow Publishing, 2019. | Series: Heredity and genetics | Audience: Grades 7 to 12.
Identifiers: LCCN 2017045148| ISBN 9780766099449 (library bound) | ISBN 9780766099456 (pbk.)
Subjects: LCSH: Microorganisms—Juvenile literature. | Microbiology—Juvenile literature. | Evolution (Biology)—Juvenile literature.
Classification: LCC QR57 .B69 2019 | DDC 579—dc23
LC record available at https://lccn.loc.gov/2017045148

Printed in the United States of America

To Our Readers: We have done our best to make sure all websites in this book were active and appropriate when we went to press. However, the author and the publisher have no control over and assume no liability for the material available on those websites or on any websites they may link to. Any comments or suggestions can be sent by email to customerservice@enslow.com.

Portions of this book appeared in *The World of Microbes: Bacteria, Viruses, and Other Microorganisms* by Janey Levy.

Contents

These rod-shaped bacteria are prokaryotes.

Introduction

There are millions of species on Earth—scientists are not sure of the exact number. It is known, however, that most of life on the planet is made up of single-celled organisms, or microbes. In fact, the first organisms on Earth were microbes. Coming in many varieties today, initially and for at least 1.5 billion years, life was composed only of prokaryotic microbes. Prokaryotes are cells that have no nuclei or organelles, which are membrane-enclosed structures that perform specific functions. Around two billion years ago, eukaryotic cells appeared. Like the cells in human bodies, eukaryotic cells do have nuclei and organelles. Single-celled prokaryotes and eukaryotes had Earth all to themselves until around seven hundred million years ago when multicellular eukaryotes became plentiful.

All of life can be divided into three domains for the purpose of classification and for revealing evolutionary relationships between organisms. Two of the domains are prokaryotic: Archaea and Bacteria. The third domain, Eukarya, includes single-celled eukaryotic organisms as well as plants, fungi (for example, mushrooms), and animals.

Archaea, bacteria, and protists, or eukaryotic microbes, are essential for the survival of all life on Earth. Without these organisms, the breakdown of wastes, including dead organisms, would stop, and this would end the recycling of nutrients for other organisms to use.

The flavor of Swiss cheese and its holes are thanks to the biochemistry of the bacteria *P. freudenreichii*.

MICROBES ADD FLAVOR TO SOME FOODS

Humans have figured out ways to take advantage of some of the biochemistry that microbes do, which people cannot, and have made them partners in the production of certain foods. It is likely that everyone eats something daily which exists thanks to the work of these helpful microbes.

The most familiar practical applications of these microbial biochemical pathways are the rising of bread and the production of beer and wine by yeast. There are many other examples: the bacteria *Lactobacillus* produces yogurt from milk; other lactobacilli produce sauerkraut from cabbage, pickles from cucumbers, and rye bread from grains and sugar. Another type of bacteria, *Acetobacter*, makes vinegar. *Propionibacterium freudenreichii* is necessary to make Swiss cheese.

The list of foods and other materials produced thanks microbes goes on and on and includes soy sauce, pumpernickel bread (and all breads), sausage, green olives, miso, kimchi, salami, buttermilk, all cheeses, chocolate, and coffee.

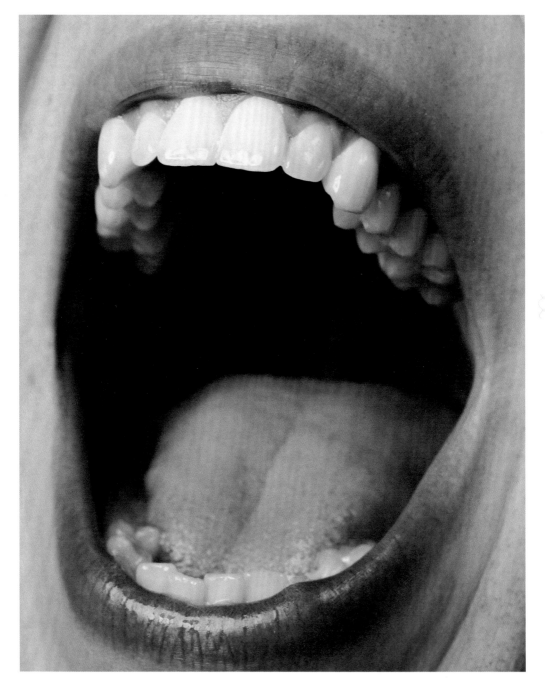

The human mouth is a welcome environment to the more than six hundred species of bacteria that live within it.

In addition to realizing the critical role microbes play for the functioning of the planet, it is also exciting to understand that microbes live in close relationship in human bodies. Consider this: the space a person's body takes up contains roughly one hundred trillion cells. Of these, only around ten trillion are actually the individual's cells. The other ninety trillion are bacteria and other single-celled organisms. In fact, if someone were to somehow remove all of "his or her" cells, these microbes would still form a clearly recognizable outline of the person's body, inside and out.

Medical researchers are beginning to study the microbes that live in and on the human body. Most of these organisms live on the skin, mouth, digestive tract (stomach and intestines), nose, throat, lungs, and urinary tract. The Human Microbiome Project is a research effort sponsored by the National Institutes of Health (NIH) that aims to figure out what species are present in the various locations of the body. Their goal is to learn about people's microbial companions in order to understand how they affect health. So far, scientists have made some quite surprising and exciting discoveries. For example, one recent study showed that there are more than 175 species of bacteria living on the forearm alone. Thirty of these species were brand new discoveries. Other regions of the skin have hundreds of other species. Scientists have discovered more than six hundred species that live in the mouth and more than seven hundred species that inhabit the large intestine. The species living in various parts of the body are different and are adapted to live in their local environment: wet, dry, oily, salty, warm, or cool.

How do these microbes in and on people's bodies affect them? Scientists are in the early stages of answering this question. So far, it is known that many of these residents appear to have no effect on humans. Others provide protection by preventing the growth of other microbes that might cause disease. And still others make people sick.

As one begins a look at microbes, taking into account their "jobs" on Earth and in human bodies, one must consider how these amazing organisms were first observed by some very surprised scientists many years ago, and how much has been learned about them.

1

How Were Microbes Discovered and Studied?

Whether prokaryotic or eukaryotic, microbes are too small to see without magnification. An entire microscopic world was hidden from view from scientists until the invention of microscopes in the seventeenth century. Prior to this breakthrough, scientists had little understanding of the basic components that make up life.

A Short History of Microscopy

The discovery and study of cells was made possible by the development and continual improvement of microscopes. In 1663 Robert Hooke (1635–1703), an English scientist, was the first to report observations of well-defined chambers in slices of cork. He called these chambers cells. Anton van Leeuwenhoek (1632–1723), a Dutch tradesman, enthusiastically explored cells, including bacteria and other microbes, through the early 1700s. His observations were so accurate that modern scientists can identify many of the organisms he studied by looking at his drawings. As microscopes improved dramatically in the nineteenth century, scientists discovered a wealth of microbial life.

As well-functioning as microscopes were in the nineteenth century, they were improved with new developments in the

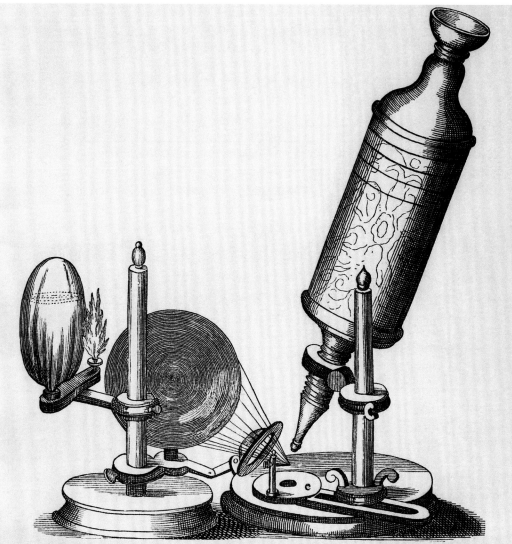

Mikroskop mit künstlicher Beleuchtung des Objektivtisches durch auffallendes Licht
aus dem Anfang des 17. Jahrhunderts

In the seventeenth century, Robert Hooke used a compound microscope that utilized light from an oil lamp passed through a water-filled glass flask to illuminate the specimen.

twentieth and twenty-first centuries. The types of microscopes developed by Hooke, van Leeuwenhoek, and others after them can do light microscopy; they depend on light to illuminate cells for viewing. Because of the physics of how lenses work with light, this type of microscopy has definite limits with respect to how much magnification is possible. In the early 1930s, a new form of microscopy, which uses a beam of electrons rather than light, permitted scientists to see cells with much greater magnification. Transmission electron microscopy allows a look at the details of the inner structure of even the smallest microbe. Scanning electron microscopy permits the examination of the surface details of microbes. Together, both forms of electron microscopy enable scientists to achieve a detailed three-dimensional view of the inside and outside of any type of cell.

Microbes and Disease

The discovery of microbes did not, at first, lead scientists and others to think there might be a connection between these organisms and illness. People had many other ideas about what caused sickness. For example, until the end of the 1800s, most believed that illnesses resulted from miasmas—bad air from swamps, dead bodies, and garbage. Some scientists and physicians pushed against this idea arguing that something physical invaded the body to produce illness. Interestingly, in 1546, the Italian physician Girolamo Fracastoro (1478–1553) had published his idea that tiny "seeds" spread infectious diseases. However, Fracastoro did not have convincing evidence to back up his claim. No one else did either.

The notion that microbes such as bacteria cause illness is known as the germ theory of disease. While Fracastoro suggested an early form of the idea, research in the 1800s addressed this

A colorized transmission electron micrograph shows cells (stained green) infected by avian influenza viruses (stained gold).

thought directly. While many scientists turned their energies to this research, the contributions of a few made history. In particular, Ignaz Semmelweis, Louis Pasteur, Robert Koch, and Joseph Lister are well remembered.

Ignaz Semmelweis

Ignaz Semmelweis (1818–1865) was a Hungarian physician. He earned his medical degree in obstetrics, the health care specialty that deals with childbirth. Semmelweis was hired to work in the maternity ward of the General Hospital in Vienna, Austria. What he observed at this hospital horrified him: a large percentage of women who came to the hospital to give birth died from a mysterious ailment, childbed fever. Semmelweis began an investigation to determine its cause.

He tested many possibilities—including miasmas—and eventually demonstrated that childbed fever was caused by "cadaverous particles" carried on the hands of physicians who had not washed thoroughly after performing autopsies, or surgical examinations, of dead patients. Semmelweis had no idea that the actual cause of childbed fever was bacteria on the physicians' hands. Nevertheless, he showed clearly that a physical material, not miasma, was responsible for this terrible infection. He also instituted hand washing rules and instructions for physicians that resulted in reducing the number of women afflicted with childbed fever.

Louis Pasteur

French chemist Louis Pasteur (1822–1895) earned his fame from his work with microbes. Credited as one of the scientists who originated the germ theory of disease, Pasteur's first work with microbes was to help wine producers figure out why their wine was going sour. Pasteur demonstrated that the vats of fermenting

Louis Pasteur was one of the microbiologists who found evidence that supported the germ theory of disease.

wine were contaminated with bacteria that produced acid. Pasteur was able to prevent this souring by a heat-killing process we now call pasteurization. This technique also became used to keep both beer and milk from going bad.

It was a logical leap from this work on wine and other foods made "sick" by bacteria to the idea that microbes could make people and other organisms sick, too. In 1879 Pasteur demonstrated that the bacterium *Bacillus anthracis* causes anthrax, thus providing evidence to support the germ theory. Two years later, he had an effective anthrax vaccine, a treatment that can prevent an infection. He began studying rabies in 1882. Unlike anthrax, rabies is caused by a virus, a microbe too small to be seen with a light microscope. Nevertheless, Pasteur figured out how to grow the virus and developed an experimental vaccine. This vaccine was put to a dramatic test when desperate parents showed up at Pasteur's door with their young son who had been attacked by a rabid dog. They begged him to save their child. Pasteur agreed to vaccinate the boy and amazingly, the child survived.

Robert Koch

Robert Koch (1843–1910) was born in the Upper Hartz Mountains region of Germany. Interested in nature and biology from childhood, Koch earned his medical degree in 1866. A skillful and effective physician, Koch was just not satisfied with the practice of medicine alone. He set up a laboratory in his four-room home and labored there for the next four years, alone, with a microscope his wife gave him as a gift and other equipment he made himself.

Independently from Pasteur, Koch performed studies that showed that anthrax was caused by a specific type of bacteria. Unlike Pasteur, Koch continued his study of anthrax bacteria and

ANTON VAN LEEUWENHOEK

Anton van Leeuwenhoek started and finished his life as a tradesman. He was born in Holland in 1632, was apprenticed to a linen draper's shop in 1648, and went into business for himself as a fabric merchant in 1654. In 1668, however, he learned how to grind lenses and make simple microscopes, and he began to look at *everything*. Some historians speculate that he was inspired by Robert Hooke's popular book *Micrographia*, which had illustrations of magnified objects.

In all, van Leeuwenhoek made more than five hundred microscopes. They opened up the previously unknown world of the very small. What did he examine and observe? To name a few examples, he scraped teeth, collected saliva, and observed the bacteria present. He examined pond water and saw tiny animals, protozoa, and single-celled green algae. After cutting himself shaving, he examined the blood on his razor and saw red blood cells. Van Leeuwenhoek wrote to the Royal Society of London, describing his discoveries. Despite his long, rambling letters and lack of formal education, the society recognized the merit of his work. He was elected as a full member in 1680, and he continued sending descriptions of his observations until the last days of his life.

was able to grow pure cultures of them for microscopic study. He photographed the bacteria and the structures they formed. Anthrax bacteria make structures, called spores, when growth conditions are poor. Koch showed that spores could germinate to create new bacterial cells. These observations solved a puzzle about anthrax: how did animals get the disease if they had not been exposed to other sick animals? The answer is that anthrax spores can remain in a resting state in the soil for years until they get the chance to infect another animal.

By 1880 Koch had developed a professional research lab— one not in his home. He developed many techniques to grow and

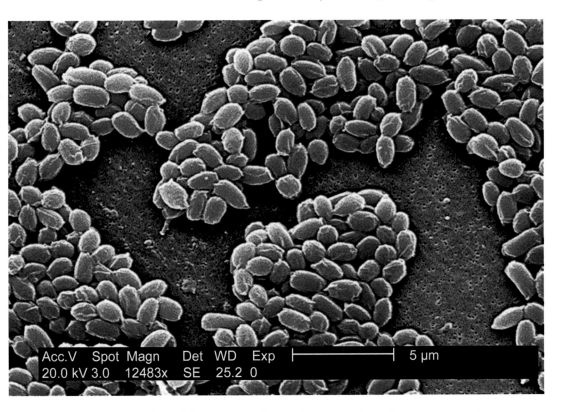

Acc.V   Spot Magn   Det WD   Exp ⊢━━━━━━━━━━━┤   5 μm
20.0 kV 3.0   12483x   SE   25.2 0

These spores produced by anthrax bacteria allow the microbe to survive harsh environmental conditions.

19

observe bacteria. Koch also traveled all over the world to figure out the identity of microbes that cause other diseases such as tuberculosis, a respiratory infection, and cholera, a disease that results in an often fatal loss of body fluids by diarrhea.

Joseph Lister

Although Semmelweis had established the importance of hand washing and cleanliness of everything that touches a patient, physicians resisted making changes in their habits and practices. The most dangerous experience for patients by far was surgery. The risk resided not only in the surgical procedures themselves, but even more in the infections that often occurred after surgery. Almost half of all patients died following surgery, even minor procedures, due to infection.

English physician Joseph Lister (1827–1912) changed that. After Pasteur's discoveries, Lister realized microbes caused infections following surgery. He insisted that antiseptics—germ-killing agents—be used on hands, instruments, and dressings (bandages). These practices immediately reduced the number of infections in surgical patients. Lister is rightly considered the "father of modern surgery."

Microbiology Today

The early history of microbiology focused a lot of attention on disease—its cause, treatment, and prevention. Even now, microbiologists and medical researchers continue to be vigilant and alert to disease threats. Infections, even deadly ones, are not things of the past. In fact, in many areas of the world, infectious disease is still a major killer.

Microbes do a lot more than cause disease, however, and so research is aimed in many other directions, too. For example, microbes are important for food production, for the treatment and prevention of disease, and for industrial applications.

As already mentioned, many foods and beverages would not exist in their familiar forms or at all without the assistance of microbes. Bread would not rise, there would be no wine or beer, many cheeses would not exist, and many pickled foods would be gone, too. With respect to disease prevention, there is a great deal of research that supports the idea that beneficial bacteria are necessary for a person's well-being. There are foods people would not be able to digest without the bacteria in the human digestive systems that help. There would be more infections of people's mouths, including tooth decay, if not for the bacteria that keep out more dangerous microbes. And a new approach is being tested for the treatment of serious infections of the large intestine, namely the transplantation of feces with healthy bacterial populations, into the intestines of an infected person. Finally, microbes are used industrially for everything from the cleanup of wastes, such as oil spills, to the production of chemicals to the development of antibiotic drugs used to combat infection.

2

What Are the Basic Ideas of Heredity and Genes?

A deep understanding of microbes, or any other organism for that matter, invites a look at genetics, the branch of biology that studies heredity and variation in organisms. The story of how microbes take in nutrients, make materials, live, and reproduce is also the story of how genes, the basic units of heredity, function. Genes are the cellular elements that influence what traits organisms, microbes or people, inherit from their parents.

Genes are located on cell structures called chromosomes. These are made of proteins and a substance called deoxyribonucleic acid, or DNA. An organism's complete set of DNA is its genome. Individual genes are DNA segments that have the information to tell the cell how to make the proteins necessary for life. For these instructions to be carried out, DNA copies or transcribes its information to produce another molecule, ribonucleic acid, or RNA. RNA, in turn, can be translated in the cell to make proteins. Proteins are the molecules that form most of the structures in cells and which are key in regulating how the cell works.

The function of a gene is widely misunderstood and often misrepresented in popular media. At its most basic, a gene is just the instructions to make a protein. The idea that there is a gene for any characteristic such as height, eye color, intelligence, race, or sexual orientation, for example, misses the mark entirely. Instead of gene *for*, one should think of genes as *used for* or *used in*. For example, one can refer to the genes used in brain development. It is also important to know that genes do not act in isolation. Their actions are influenced by other genes, the environment, and even chance.

A Short History of Genetics

People want to know where they came from and why they look and act the way they do. Humans have been interested in how heredity works since at least the dawn of agriculture. Plant breeding for crop improvement and animal breeding to increase milk yield, strength, or meat production were practiced long before anyone had a clue about the mechanisms responsible for these successes. People developed significant practical knowledge regarding breeding, and for most, this was all a person needed to know. However, as is true in all time periods and places, there were some individuals who were seized by the need to know *how* a thing works. They wanted to understand the exact mechanisms of inheritance.

The first major figure who opened up the door to a modern experimental investigation of heredity was Gregor Mendel (1822–1884), an Augustinian monk from the Brunn Monastery (in what is now the Czech Republic). Mendel's experiments on the heredity of traits in pea plants led him to work out the basic rules governing how information is passed from one generation to the next. Mendel published his work in 1866, but it went largely unnoticed until 1900 when other scientists who had done

MENDELIAN INHERITANCE

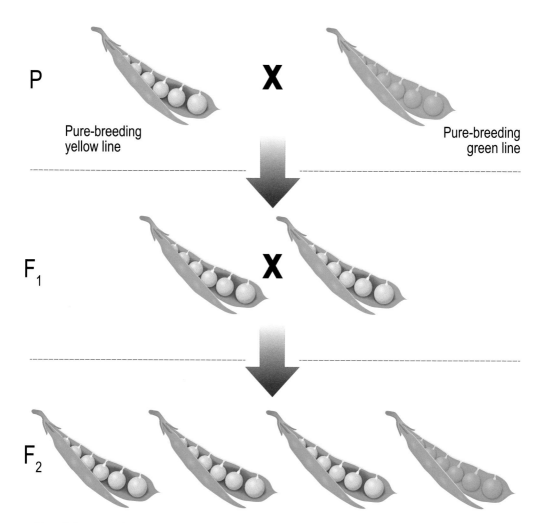

P
Pure-breeding yellow line
X
Pure-breeding green line

F_1
X

F_2

Mendel crossed a yellow-seed producing plant with a green-seed producing plant (P). All of the offspring had yellow seeds (F1). When the yellow seed plant was crossed with itself, three out of four offspring had yellow seeds, while one had green seeds (F2). This showed that some traits (yellow seeds) were dominant, or physically expressed, while others were recessive (green seeds), or masked, yet still present in the genes.

similar experiments found Mendel's paper as they prepared their own publications.

Many scientists performed experiments to study the patterns of inheritance in a lot of different organisms. Organisms were mated and data were collected on the characteristics of the offspring. More and more was learned about the details of how traits were passed on from one generation to the next. However, at this point, there was really no understanding at all about the physical nature of genes. Where were they located? What were they made of?

In most eukaryotic organisms, such as the peas that Mendel studied, reproduction and the development of offspring depend on the production of gametes, or sex cells. In animals, gametes are sperm and eggs. The type of cell division, meiosis, that produced gametes was first observed and described in the late 1800s. Meiosis separates the chromosomes, the structures where genes are located, into the gametes so that each cell gets a full set of instructions for inheritance. While the relationship between chromosomes and genes is understood today, it was a mystery during the early days of genetic research.

This all changed thanks to several scientists but especially T. H. Morgan. A biologist at Columbia University in New York City, Morgan studied fruit fly genetics. This might seem odd—why care about fruit flies? Morgan chose fruit flies because they are easy to grow and manipulate for experimentation. Also they did not cost much to maintain. Morgan and his students did some critical studies that demonstrated that genes were in fact on chromosomes. They showed, for example, that the behavior of chromosomes in meiosis was similar to the behavior and sorting of the genes that produced physical characteristics in their genetic crosses of fruit flies. Morgan's team was even able to construct the

A CLOSER LOOK AT MEIOSIS

During Prophase I, the nuclear membrane disappears, DNA forms into chromosomes, and structures called centrioles begin to migrate to opposite poles of the cell. In Metaphase I, homologous (matching) pairs of chromosomes find each other and line up side by side, one on either side of the cell's centerline. Spindle fibers stretch from each centromere to the centrioles of the two poles. In Anaphase I, the paired chromosomes move apart and go toward opposite sides of the cell. In Telophase I, nuclear membranes form around the two new sets of chromosomes, and there are two new cells, each with half the number of chromosomes that was in the original cell.

During Prophase II, each of the two cell's DNA molecules coil into chromosomes again. In Metaphase II, the centromeres of all the chromosomes line up in single file down the center of the cell. Spindle fibers stretch between each centromere and the two centrioles located at opposite poles of the cell. During Anaphase II, centromeres break apart and separate the two parts of the chromosome called chromatids. A spindle fiber from the centriole attaches to each centromere and pulls it away from the middle of the cell. During Telophase II, the two sets of DNA have completely separated from each other and a new nuclear membrane forms around each set. Each of the new four cells gets one chromosome (a single chromatid with one copy of the DNA) for each homologous pair in the original cell.

MEIOSIS

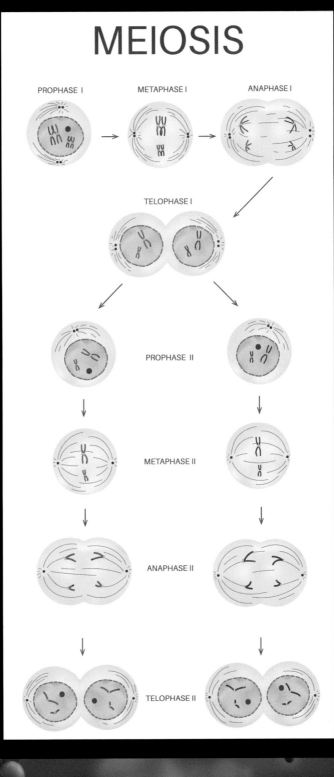

PROPHASE I   METAPHASE I   ANAPHASE I

TELOPHASE I

PROPHASE II

METAPHASE II

ANAPHASE II

TELOPHASE II

Gametes, such as eggs and sperm, reproduce by meiosis. The process results in four cells.

first genetic maps in which they could identify where genes were located on specific chromosomes.

Morgan's work was just the beginning of an explosion in genetic research that led to the understanding of the biochemistry and molecular biology of inheritance, too. For example, in the 1940s, biologist George W. Beadle and biochemist Edward L. Tatum demonstrated how genes work. Their experiments on a mold (a kind of fungus) showed genes that direct the production of a particular type of protein, called an enzyme, which controls chemical reactions in cells. In fact, these scientists established that *each gene* controls the production of *one specific enzyme*. Yet a question remained: which material in chromosomes made up the genes?

Discovering DNA

Scientists isolated nucleic acids, DNA and RNA, from nuclei in the nineteenth century. In 1869 physician and biologist Johann Friedrich Miescher isolated DNA alone. However, other scientists had shown that nuclei are also good sources of protein. So while scientists had a sense that nuclei were important in inheritance, the common view was that it would be protein, a much more structurally complex molecule than DNA, which would be the material of inheritance. DNA simply did not seem like a good bet. This view prevailed until 1944, when Oswald Avery, Colin MacLoed, and Maclyn McCarty were able to take isolated DNA from one variety of bacteria and change the physical characteristics of another variety of bacteria that took this foreign DNA into their cells. Astonishingly, these transformed or altered bacteria passed on their new traits to their offspring. They were permanently changed.

So what exactly is DNA? It's composed of chemical building blocks called nucleotides. Nucleotides contain three components: a phosphate group, a sugar (deoxyribose), and a base. Since all nucleotides are identical except for their bases, scientists identify them by their base. The four DNA bases are adenine (A), guanine (G), thymine (T), and cytosine (C).

In 1953 biologists James Watson and Francis Crick proposed that DNA is a double helix, which resembles a ladder twisted into a spiral. The phosphate and sugar molecules are connected by strong chemical bonds and form the strong sides of the ladder. The bases form the rungs and are connected to one another by numerous relatively weak chemical bonds. Chemical rules govern how the bases bond. Adenine always bonds with thymine; guanine always bonds with cytosine.

Cracking the Genetic Code

By 1953 scientists knew genes were bits of DNA and probably carried a code that tells the cell how to make proteins. However, they couldn't read the code. By 1961 scientists had determined that the nucleotides in DNA were arranged in groups of three, which they called codons. Each codon instructs the cell to insert a specific amino acid, one of the building blocks of proteins. Scientists then set out to determine which codon corresponds to which amino acid. In essence, they wished to determine how the cell translates the language of nucleotides to that of amino acids. The first identification of a codon and its amino acid was achieved by the biochemist Marshall Nirenberg. In quick succession, scientists identified the codons for all twenty amino acids found in the proteins of living organisms. Consequently, scientists had the key to begin unlocking the mystery of each gene's function.

Rosalind Franklin is pictured here in 1955. Her work was essential for the discovery of DNA's structure.

ROSALIND FRANKLIN

While Watson and Crick are the names most closely associated with discovering the structure of DNA, their breakthrough actually depended on the research of the English chemist Rosalind Franklin (1920–1958). A brilliant student, Franklin earned her PhD in 1945 and embarked on a successful research career when few women did. She became an expert in a technique called X-ray crystallography, a method that allows scientists to visualize structural features of molecules.

In 1951, Franklin was hired to work at Kings College in London specifically to study DNA. She learned a lot about the structure of DNA including its double stranded nature, that it has a sugar phosphate backbone on the outside, and has bases paired on the inside. She had not yet figured out how the bases were paired.

Unbeknownst to Franklin, another scientist showed her data to Watson and Crick. They took what they had learned in their research, combined it with the information from Franklin, and figured out the structure of DNA. She never knew what had happened. In 1962 Watson and Crick were awarded Nobel Prizes for their work. Sadly, Franklin died in 1958 and did not get the recognition she deserved in her lifetime for her essential part in the discovery of DNA's structure.

DNA double helix

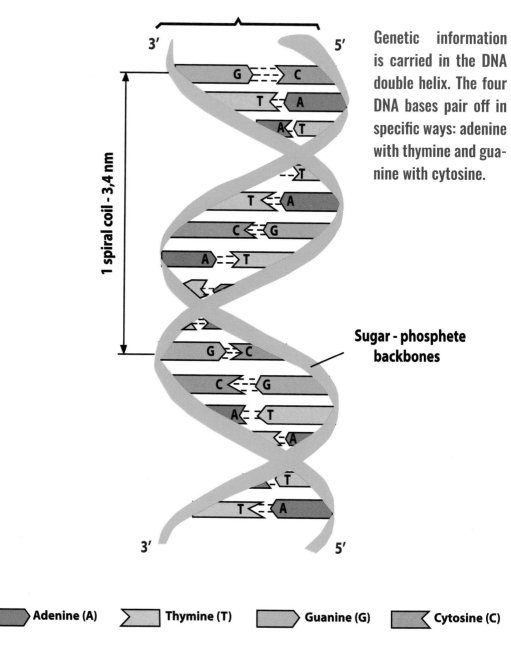

Genetic information is carried in the DNA double helix. The four DNA bases pair off in specific ways: adenine with thymine and guanine with cytosine.

1 spiral coil - 3,4 nm

Sugar - phosphete backbones

Adenine (A)　　Thymine (T)　　Guanine (G)　　Cytosine (C)

32

Inheritance and Reproduction

Two basic types of reproduction exist—asexual and sexual. With asexual reproduction, the offspring are identical and, unless there is a genetic error or mutation, they possess the exact same genes as the parent cells. With sexual reproduction, cells exchange and combine genetic information with a partner. Many microbes, including archaea, bacteria, and protists, generally reproduce asexually, although many have ways to exchange genetic material with others of their species (and sometimes with organisms of different species). The exchange of genetic material is a microbial version of sexual reproduction. Some protists, or single-celled eukaryotes, have life cycles wherein they undergo actual sexual reproduction complete with specialized sex cells.

3

What Are the Important Features of Prokaryotes?

All life on Earth descended from a common single-celled, anaerobic prokaryotic ancestor. Anaerobic organisms live in the absence of oxygen. The early Earth did not have much free oxygen. This first cell originated at least 3.5 billion years ago. Scientists are not entirely sure when the Archaea and Bacteria domains split from each other because the shape and size of the two types of prokaryotic cells are so similar, making it hard to distinguish between fossil versions of these cells. Most scientists think, however, that the separation happened very early, near the dawn of life itself. Cells from both domains have a lot in common:

- They are small, generally no more than 0.5 to 5 μm in length. (A period at the end of a sentence is 1000 μm wide.)
- They live most often as single cells.
- They contain a single circular chromosome that is not enclosed in a membrane.
- They do not possess membrane-bound organelles.
- They are enclosed by a cell membrane and cell wall.
- They are found in every environment on Earth including some that would seem hostile to life.

Bacteria Cell Anatomy

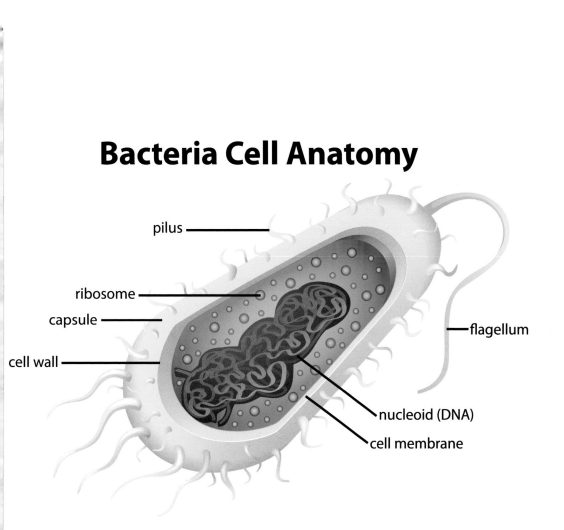

pilus

ribosome

capsule

cell wall

flagellum

nucleoid (DNA)

cell membrane

This diagram shows the internal and external structures of a bacterial cell.

Prokaryotes are essential for the functioning of all life on Earth. If these highly successful organisms were to disappear, all the living things in the world would perish. The reverse is not true—if all humans, for example, ceased to exist, archaea and bacteria would continue to thrive as they have done for billions of years.

Prokaryotes are diverse groups of organisms; scientists are not even sure how many species there are. To make sense of the vast array of these organisms, one can consider their biology and in particular three questions:

- What challenges and opportunities do prokaryotes face in the microscopic world they inhabit?
- How do prokaryotes reproduce?
- How do prokaryotes get food and energy?

Prokaryotic Challenges and Opportunities

Single-celled and tiny, prokaryotic cells encounter a physical world that is different from the one humans experience. Because they are so small, the cells are not very sensitive to gravity. For example, when a person sneezes, millions of bacteria are expelled into the air where they can remain suspended and thus spread on a breeze or on air movement of any sort. However, prokaryotic cells are affected by the forces of friction that exist between them and their environments. For instance, prokaryotic cells experience challenges in trying to move through fluids. Imagine what it is like to walk through water. Now, imagine walking through molasses. A prokaryotic cell moving through water experiences frictional forces more similar to what someone would encounter if he or she were trying to walk through molasses. Prokaryotic cells attempting to move through even thicker material, such as

SPONTANEOUS GENERATION

If anyone has ever had the unpleasant experience of coming across a dead animal in the woods or on the side of the road, he or she probably noticed that the carcass was covered with maggots. Most people would find this observation startling or even disgusting. Yet one would not conclude that the dead animal had "turned into" maggots. People in ancient times, however, believed that maggots arose "spontaneously" and directly from an animal's remains. It is known today that the only way new individuals arise is from their parents, through reproduction. This is true not just for multicellular animals like maggots, but for microbes, too. How was this result established scientifically?

Louis Pasteur performed the critical experiment that demonstrated that life comes only from the reproduction of other living organisms. Pasteur cultured bacteria in S-shaped glass flasks. He poured culture broth into these "swan-neck" flasks and then boiled the broth to sterilize it; no bacteria remained. The flasks were left open to the air, but because of the S-shaped neck, dust particles could not fall into the flask. As a consequence, even though air could enter, no bacteria did. The broth remained sterile. When Pasteur broke off the neck, so that the broth was directly under the opening of the flask, a teeming population of bacteria appeared within a day. Although Pasteur was not the only scientist to address whether microorganisms could generate spontaneously, his experiment was so decisive that it put to rest the question of spontaneous generation, once and for all.

mucus, have an even harder time. This physical challenge, due to their size, presents problems for prokaryotic cells including how to obtain food or position themselves in environments that support survival.

The solution to the challenge of friction is that many prokaryotes are motile meaning they are able to move or locomote. One of the most common mechanisms of motility in prokaryotic cells is swimming powered by flagellar movement. The stiff, bent, rod-like flagella on prokaryotic cells spin like a boat propeller and move the cells through their surroundings. In the absence of an attractant, such as food, or a repellent, such as a noxious material or poison, prokaryotic cells swim in random directions. When they encounter food or a repellent, prokaryotic cells alter the behavior of their flagella and swim toward the attractant or away from the repellent. Even though the size of prokaryotic cells means that they experience their physical world differently than the way that humans and other large animals do, they are still highly functional.

Prokaryotic Reproduction

Prokaryotic cells reproduce primarily by binary fission. In this process, the DNA copies itself, the cell grows, and the cell splits into two. Each daughter cell receives the gel-like cytoplasm and one complete chromosome. Binary fission happens rapidly; thus, prokaryotic cells can easily achieve population booms. Depending upon conditions, cells can divide every one to three hours. Under ideal conditions in a laboratory setting, some species can divide every twenty minutes.

Binary fission is a highly effective way to generate a large population of cells quickly. However, because binary fission results in identical copies of cells, there is no source of genetic diversity,

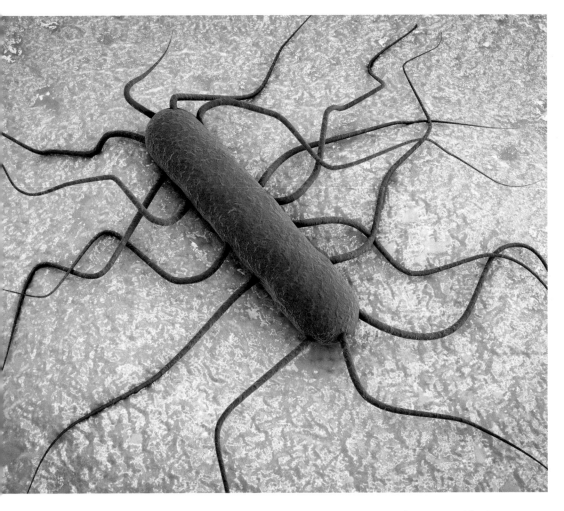

The rod-like flagella on this bacterium, *Listeria monocytogenes*, enable it to swim.

except for what mutation, or a change in DNA, introduces. While mutation is a source of genetic diversity, prokaryotic cells also have three mechanisms available for the exchange of genetic material with other cells: transformation, conjugation, and transduction.

Genetic material released into the environment by other cells can be taken in by the process of transformation. With conjugation, two prokaryotic cells connect physically to one another by a tube through which genetic material can pass. And through the process of transduction, genes can also be passed from one cell to another by viruses, microbes that are not cells themselves and which cannot survive and reproduce outside of a cell.

How Do Prokaryotes Get Food and Energy?

Perhaps the most astonishing feature of prokaryotes as a group is their ability to grow and thrive in a range of environments, including some that at first glance would appear inhospitable to life. This capacity for growth and survival just about anywhere is thanks to the ability of prokaryotes, as a group, to extract and use energy from so many different types of material. Prokaryotes display a biochemical diversity far beyond that of all other groups of organisms combined.

Because prokaryotic cells are small, they cannot "eat" in the sense of bringing large bits of food into their cells. Instead, they rely on the transport of molecules across the wall and membrane that cover each cell. All prokaryotic cells require a source of energy and a source of carbon. Prokaryotes, therefore, can be organized into four categories based on their styles of getting nutrition and their sources of carbon and energy: photoautotrophs, photoheterotrophs, chemoautotrophs, and chemoheterotrophs.

Photoautotrophs use sunlight as an energy source and the gas carbon dioxide as a carbon source. They use energy from the sun to produce sugar from carbon dioxide, thereby photosynthesizing like plants do. All organisms that breathe release carbon dioxide so this is a plentiful material. Cyanobacteria are an example of prokaryotes that photosynthesize.

Cyanobacteria and other photoautotrophs actually changed the conditions of the early Earth by producing oxygen. As oxygen increased in the environment, some organisms died because oxygen was deadly to them. Other organisms, including humanity's ancestors, survived. Humans and many other types of organisms require oxygen to live.

In addition, this oxygen produced ozone that eventually made a protective layer in the atmosphere, blocking the transmission of ultraviolet (UV) light from the sun. UV light damages nucleic acids, so by preventing excessive exposure to UV irradiation, ozone protected organisms from life-threatening DNA.

Besides being photosynthetic, cyanobacteria take nitrogen gas from the air and convert that gas into nitrogen-containing molecules that organisms, such as plants, can use—a process known as nitrogen fixation. Prokaryotic cells play an essential role in nitrogen cycling, which refers to the overall movement of nitrogen through the environment. Organisms take in and use nitrogen that has been fixed by bacteria (in the case of animals, by eating plants and/or animals). Organisms then dispose of the nitrogen through waste and decomposition (after death), which releases nitrogen back into the soil. Different types of bacteria then extract nitrogen from the waste products in the soil, producing compounds that release nitrogen back into the atmosphere. Life on Earth depends on nitrogen cycling, and only some prokaryotes, such as cyanobacteria, have the ability to do it. Eukaryotic cells are unable to fix nitrogen.

The dark clusters of small cells are cyanobacteria in front of long eukaryotic cells arranged in rings.

Photoheterotrophs use sunlight as their energy source, but they require carbon from a more complex molecule, such as sugar, rather than from carbon dioxide. *Rhodopseudomonas* (purple nonsulfar bacteria) are one such example. Only prokaryotes use this nutritional mode.

In another type of nutrition that is unique to prokaryotes, chemoautotrophs extract energy from substances such as hydrogen, hydrogen sulfide, or iron, instead of sunlight. However, like photoautotrophs, chemoautotrophs use carbon dioxide as their carbon source. *Thiomicrospira crunogena*, the prokaryotes found in very harsh environments like the deep sea, are one such example.

Finally, chemoheterotrophs use organic food molecules, such as sugar, for both their energy and carbon sources. This mode of nutrition is not unique to prokaryotes. In fact, this is a common way for organisms to obtain nutrition. All multicellular non-photosynthetic organisms, such as animals, use this nutritional mode. *Escherichia coli* (*E. coli*), a common gut bacterium used widely in research, is an example of a chemoheterotroph.

The biochemical diversity of prokaryotic cells has some practical consequences in the environment. First, prokaryotes play an essential role in the decomposition of wastes, such as dead organisms. Second, they are critical for the functioning of the carbon, oxygen, and nitrogen cycles. All life depends on the back and forth flow of these materials between organisms and the environment. Finally, the capacity of prokaryotes as a group to grow on just about anything makes them ideal for cleaning up pollutants such as oil spills or heavy metal residues produced by industry.

When considering prokaryotes as a whole, it is easy to risk focusing too much attention on their size and relatively simple

This scanning electron micrograph shows *E. coli* in red.

structure when compared to eukaryotic organisms. But to do so misses an important point: prokaryotes were the first organisms on Earth, and they remain highly successful and the most abundant. By biomass, meaning how much organisms weigh, living prokaryotes outweigh the total biomass of *all* other organisms on Earth. Prokaryotic cells were the first to use the biochemical pathways that are present in eukaryotic cells today.

How Do Bacteria and Archaea Compare?

Although Archaea and Bacteria domains are both prokaryotic, molecular and biochemical evidence make it clear that Archaea are more closely related to Eukarya, the eukaryotic domain, than they are to Bacteria. Originally characterized as bacteria, because they look so visually similar, in the 1970s a closer inspection of the DNA of what were then called archaebacteria revealed that these cells differed from bacteria in terms of the chemistry of the cell membrane, cell wall, ribosomes (the structures in cells that assemble amino acids into proteins), RNA polymerase (the enzyme that makes RNA), and even flagella:

- The cell membranes of bacteria contain fatty acid molecules, while those of archaea contain another type of lipid molecule called isoprene.
- Bacterial cell walls contain a structural component called peptidoglycans, while archaea do not possess this structural substance.
- Bacterial ribosomes are shaped differently than the ribosomes in archaea.
- Bacteria contain a simple type of RNA polymerase, while the RNA polymerase found in archaea more closely resembles RNA polymerase found in eukaryotic cells.

- The flagella of bacteria grow from the tip, while the flagella of archaea grow from the bottom.

Some of the first archaea identified were species that live in extreme environments such as near deep-sea vents, in high temperature bodies of water, in acidic water, and in concentrated saline. These are all places that bacteria cannot grow. Because of their ability to grow in such inhospitable environments, which are similar to the physical conditions in some industries, archaea show a lot of promise for helping with the cleanup of pollutants and industrial waste.

More recent research has revealed that arcahaea are also alsoabundant in less extreme environments, places where bacteria are also found. In fact, archaea are important occupants living in the digestive systems of many animals, including humans. Many of the archaeal species present in the gut are methanogens; they aid in digestion and produce methane as a byproduct.

Human bodies have an intimate relationship with both archaea and bacteria—thousands of species live on and in them. Many of these organisms are actually quite helpful to humans. Some keep the growth of harmful bacteria in check. Others make it easier for people to digest foods they would have trouble handling alone. Nevertheless, some bacteria cause serious and even fatal diseases. Interestingly, there are no known pathogenic archaea. Scientists are not sure why archaea and bacteria differ in this regard.

4

How Did Eukaryotic Cells Originate?

rokaryotic cells, both bacteria and archaea, had the whole planet to themselves for close to two billion years. Eukaryotes appeared on Earth between 1.8 and 1.9 billion years ago. If one were to look at the history of life and consider that prokaryotes have been here for 100 percent of the time, eukaryotes have existed for only 53 percent. And multicellular animals, having appeared approximately 580 million years ago, have existed for only 16 percent. While prokaryotes have dominated, their structure and functional characteristics—in particular their size—do limit what they are able to do.

Size Challenges of Prokaryotes

Because entry of materials such as food molecules and exit of wastes depend on the cell membrane, the size of prokaryotic cells is limited by the amount of surface area available. As a cell gets bigger, the volume increases at a greater rate than the surface area. Surface area refers to how much area is exposed on the surface of an object. Eventually, the needs of the interior of the cell cannot be met by the moving of materials across the available surface area. Therefore, prokaryotic cells were limited in how large they could become and survive.

The much larger tan-colored protozoan cell is eating smaller eukaryotic cells called diatoms (colored blue)

As a result of these size limitations, any cells that evolved traits allowing for an increase in size would have had a tremendous advantage and would have opportunities not available to prokaryotic cells. For example, if a cell became large enough, it could eat other smaller cells. In addition, genomes could increase in size, meaning that more different types of proteins could be made. Since proteins are responsible for the structure and function of organisms, a larger genome would allow for greater complexity. Consider, for example, how much more complex human bodies are than a bacterial cell. Some of this difference is due to a larger genome.

How Did Eukaryotes Evolve?

Evidence points to two parallel events that led to the evolution of prokaryotic cells into eukaryotic cells. First, the plasma membrane in a prokaryotic cell infolded, surrounded the chromosome, and formed a nucleus. These membrane infoldings gave rise to many of the membrane bound organelles of eukaryotic cells. Second, prokaryotic cells (that probably lacked cell walls) ate other prokaryotic cells, and the engulfed prokaryotic cells became mitochondria, the organelles that break down food molecules to produce energy. Rather than dying, these engulfed bacteria entered into a symbiotic relationship with their host. In a symbiotic relationship, both the host cell and engulfed bacteria benefit. Eventually, the host and engulfed bacteria became mutually dependent and unable to live without each other. Finally, and occurring much later in the history of life, a host cell ate cyanobacteria. These cyanobacteria survived, became essential to the survival of the host, and ultimately became chloroplasts, the organelles responsible for photosynthesis.

INCREASING THE SURFACE AREA OF THE CIRCULATORY SYSTEM

The surface area challenge that cells face as they get bigger is not unique to them. Large animals, such as humans, need to get oxygen and food into each cell of the body. They also need to remove wastes from cells. Yet most cells are very far from the surface of the body. How is this problem solved?

The circulatory system is the body's system that brings blood to each cell. It consists of a series of vessels, larger ones that branch and branch again into ever smaller and more numerous vessels, until the vessels become small enough and numerous enough to reach every cell. Branching structures are a common feature in organisms. They dramatically increases the total surface area of the structures. When oxygen or food molecules move from the bloodstream to the cells, they must cross the surface of a blood vessel. A larger surface area means more room for the transfer—meaning more oxygen and food molecules are delivered and more waste products are removed.

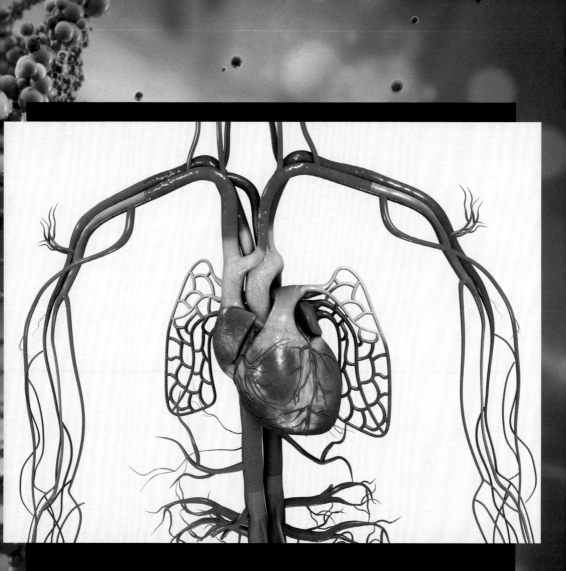

The branching blood vessels increase the total surface area of the circulatory system. Arteries (*red*) branch into arterioles while veins branch into venules. Both arterioles and venules, in turn, lead to capillaries that exchange materials, such as oxygen, nutrients, and waste, between blood and the surrounding tissue.

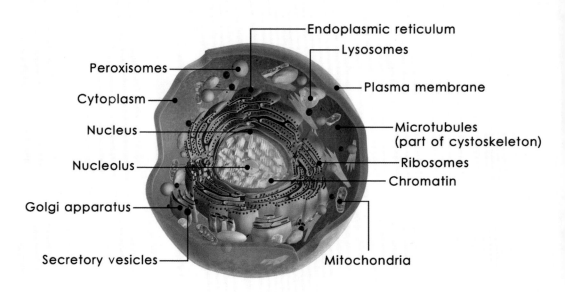

Peroxisomes

Cytoplasm

Nucleus

Nucleolus

Golgi apparatus

Secretory vesicles

Endoplasmic reticulum

Lysosomes

Plasma membrane

Microtubules (part of cystoskeleton)

Ribosomes

Chromatin

Mitochondria

This cross section of a eukaryotic cell reveals its internal structures.

There is a lot of evidence that supports this scenario of eukaryotic cell evolution. First, some present-day prokaryotes *do* have modest infoldings of their membranes into the interior of cells. Second, mitochondria and chloroplasts have characteristics similar to prokaryotic cells. Both of these organelles

- possess circular chromosomes of their own (bacteria have circular chromosomes)
- contain ribosomes that are structured similarly to those found in bacteria (and unlike the ones found in eukaryotic cells)

- reproduce by binary fission (like bacteria do)
- contain two outer membranes, the internal one of which is similar biochemically to bacterial cell membranes

Most scientists think that the host cells were archaea; the bacteria engulfed that became mitochondria were aerobic, meaning they lived in oxygen-rich environments. The ancestors of chloroplasts were oxygen-producing bacterial cells, similar to cyanobacteria.

Examination of eukaryotic genes that are important for DNA replication, the production of RNA, and the synthesis of proteins reveal close similarities to archaeal genes. However, some eukaryotic genes important for certain biochemical processes are similar to those found in bacteria. These genetic differences point to the fact that eukaryotic cells come from a combination of both bacteria and archaea.

5

What Are the Important Features of Protists?

Eukaryotic organisms that live all or most of their lives as single cells are called protists. Protists as a group are extremely diverse. In a sense, they represent "evolutionary experimentation" regarding how to be a eukaryotic cell. They display several evolutionary trends: increased size, increased complexity, and even hints at the development of multicellularity. The basic structures, behaviors, and capacities of these cells are seen in cells of multicellular organisms, too. While interesting in their own right, learning about protists also provides important insights about all eukaryotic cells and for this reason many of these species are used as model organisms in research exploring all sorts of questions about cells.

At one time, scientists thought that protists all belonged together in one kingdom. More recent research, however, has shown that protists are not all closely related. In fact, some taxonomists, scientists who are experts in the classification of organisms, argue that protist is a category of convenience and that there are actually *many* kingdoms of protists. In other words, many experts say that along with the animal, plant, and fungal kingdoms, there are multiple separate kingdoms made up entirely by different groups of protists. And, just because protists are, for the most part, unicellular, this does not mean they are all close relatives.

It is quite challenging to categorize protists, which makes taxonomy of protists a very active area of research in which there is a lot of disagreement. Rather than wade into the details, one can just look at some representative protists and consider three descriptive, informal categories of protists: animal-like, plant-like, and fungal-like and address how they eat, reproduce, and behave.

Protozoa: Animal-like Protists

Sometimes called protozoa, animal-like protists live by eating or ingesting food—they are little hunters. They are motile and highly sensitive to their environments. Two examples are amoebae and ciliates.

Amoebae

From a structural perspective, amoebae are amongst the simplest protozoa. They are perhaps the most ancient eukaryotic cell. Lacking structures that propel cells, such as flagella, amoebae move by extending parts of their bodies as pseudopods. The cytoplasm in the cell flows in the direction of the pseudopod and the entire cell oozes like a little blob of viscous goo. The cytoskeleton, a series of fibers and motor proteins present in eukaryotic cells, is essential for cell movement. Amoeboid movement is also used by certain cells in human bodies—white blood cells of the immune system for example.

Amoebae are capable of detecting attractants such as food, or repellents such as poisons. Pseudopods will bulge in the direction of food. Upon reaching the food, the amoebae will engulf it. Ultimately, the food ends up inside the cell for digestion.

An amoeba is an example of a structurally simple eukaryotic cell. The pseudopods help it move and feed.

WHITE BLOOD CELLS: THE AMOEBAE IN HUMAN BODIES

The tasks that the cells in human bodies are able to do and the ways they behave were all first worked out by ancient protists long ago. Macrophages, a type of protective cell in the immune system, help to fight infections.

Located all over the body, macrophages will leave the bloodstream and crawl, like the amoeboid cells they are, into areas where there is infection or cellular damage. Once there, macrophages will eat anything that does not belong—dead cells, microbes, debris, dirt, and even cancer cells.

Amoebae reproduce asexually; mitosis makes identical daughter cells. This is the predominant form of reproduction for many amoeba species. In fact, until quite recently, most scientists thought amoebae were not capable of sexual reproduction. Recent research has revealed that amoebae can indeed generate genetic diversity through sexual reproduction.

To summarize the day-to-day life of an amoeba, presuming it avoids being eaten: the amoeba crawls slowly in search of food and makes more amoebae generally by mitosis.

Ciliates

Ciliates, in contrast to amoebae, are probably the most structurally elaborate and complex of the protists. Most ciliates

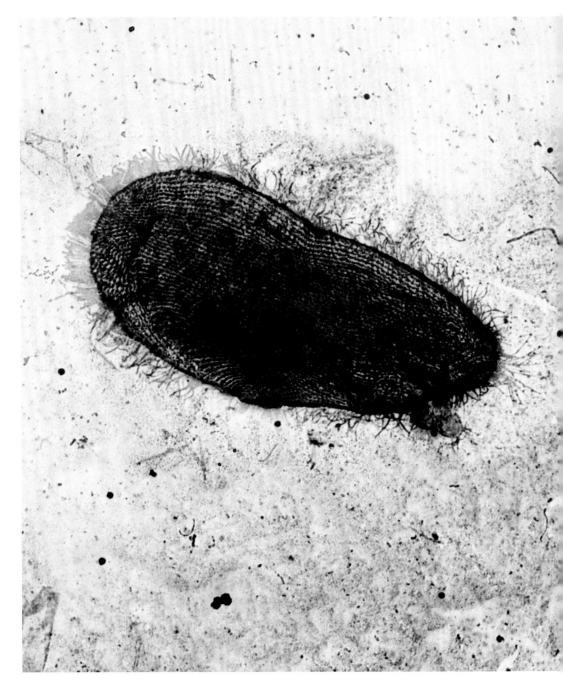

A paramecium is an example of a structurally complex eukaryotic cell.

live in water and swim using cilia, which are like flagella found on some eukaryotic cells such as sperm, but are shorter and more numerous. Depending upon the species, the arrangement of cilia can be complicated. Consider a paramecium as an example. This cell is covered with rows of cilia that coordinate movement like the oars on a boat.

A paramecium is a fast swimmer. Because it is so much bigger than a prokaryotic cell, a paramecium experiences less frictional force when swimming through water. They are highly sensitive to the environment and can maneuver skillfully to capture food or avoid harmful situations. Like amoebae, paramecia reproduce asexually by mitosis. However, unlike most amoebae, paramecia can also undergo sexual reproduction in which cells of different mating types fuse temporarily, exchange genetic material, and then undergo division to produce daughter cells with new combinations of genes contributed by parent cells.

Green Algae: Plant-like Protists

Green algae serve as a good example for plant-like protists. Thought to be the ancestors of plants, green algae are photosynthetic cells. They possess chloroplasts very similar in structure to those seen in plants. Also like plant cells, green algae have cell walls.

Chlamydomonas is a specific example of photosynthetic green algae. *Chlamydomonas* possesses two flagella that coordinate movement for swimming to desirable environments, such as those with the right amount of sunlight. With respect to reproduction, *Chlamydomonas* can reproduce asexually or sexually. With asexual reproduction, cells undergo mitosis and produce identical daughter cells. Sexual reproduction involves the fusion of cells of opposite mating types to produce a zygote—the single-celled

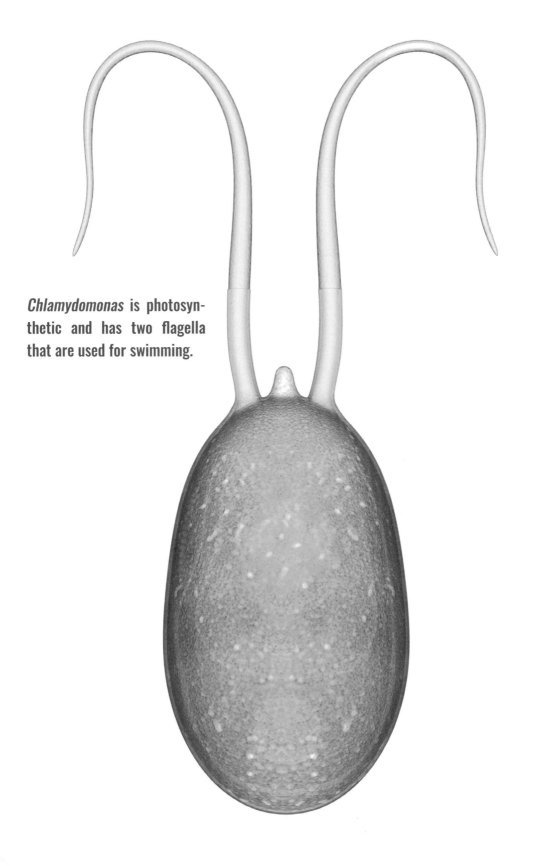

Chlamydomonas is photosynthetic and has two flagella that are used for swimming.

first stage of offspring with a new set of genes contributed by the parent cells. The zygote itself divides and makes new cells.

Slime Molds: Fungal-like Protists

Fungal-like protists are an extremely interesting and unusual group of organisms because they spend part of their life cycles single-celled and another part in multicellular forms. They exhibit complex life cycles and a greater degree of functional and structural division of labor than seen in other protists. Division of labor means that somewhat specialized cells do particular jobs rather than having each cell do *everything*. Two examples are plasmodial slime molds and cellular slime molds.

Plasmodial Slime Molds

Plasmodial slime molds are practically the creatures of science fiction. The feeding stage is a motile blob that can get bigger than several square meters in diameter in some species. Depending on its size, this feeding stage, or plasmodium, contains hundreds to many thousands of nuclei. Plasmodia crawl in search of food and to avoid light or other conditions where they might dry out. The movement of plasmodia is powered by a cytoplasmic flow that depends on a functional cytoskeleton—similar to amoeboid movement, but on a much bigger scale.

Plasmodia engulf food and reproduce asexually by making more nuclei through mitosis. But there is no division of the cell body, so the plasmodium gets bigger with the cell membrane enclosing the multiple nuclei within. In many respects, the plasmodium is a giant cell.

When environmental conditions deteriorate—no food, too dry, too light—plasmodial slime molds can shift to sexual development. They produce fruiting bodies that include resting

This yellow blob is a slime mold plasmodium called Mycetozoa.

structures called spores positioned on top of a stalk. When environmental conditions improve, the spores germinate and the cells they release form new plasmodia.

Cellular Slime Molds

Cellular slime molds also have a complex life cycle. They have a feeding stage in which individual amoeboid cells called myxamoebae are more or less independent of each other. These cells eat by engulfing food and move by amoeboid motion. Cellular slime molds reproduce asexually by mitosis. When food becomes unavailable or if environmental conditions become unfavorable, the myxamoebae communicate with each other using a chemical signal that causes them to gather together and construct a multicellular organism. Ultimately, a fruiting body forms with spores on top of a delicate stalk. Once conditions are

Shown here are cellular slime mold fruiting bodies from *Dictyostelium discoideum* in various stages of their formation.

suitable for growth, spores germinate and liberate the myxamoebae so the asexual life cycle can resume.

Cellular slime molds also have a sexual pathway in which myxamoebae of opposite mating types fuse to form a resistant resting structure called a macrocyst. As is true of the asexually produced spores, macrocysts germinate to release myxamoebae once environmental conditions are welcoming for growth.

6

What Microbes Bridge the Gap Between Living and Non-living?

There are two types of microbes that are not even alive or capable of independent existence: viruses and prions. Viruses, particles that bridge the gap between living and nonliving, cannot replicate unless they are inside a host cell. Viruses have a shell or coat made of protein, and genetic material within. Viruses may contain DNA, like living cells do, *or* RNA. Some viruses have an additional protective envelope of proteins, fats, and carbohydrates surrounding the coat. Some envelopes have spike-like structures that help the virus attach to host cells. In order to replicate, the virus must invade the host's cells. Once there, viruses pirate the host's biochemical machinery, turning it to the task of making virus proteins, nucleic acids, and ultimately viruses. While not all viruses cause sickness, specific types are responsible for many diseases including AIDS (acquired immune-deficiency syndrome), chicken pox, and even the common cold.

How Do Viruses Work?

Most viruses infect only specific host cells. A virus recognizes its host through receptor molecules on the host's cell membrane. Receptors help the virus bind to the host. Depending on the

This scanning electron micrograph shows HIV (colored pink) budding from the surface of infected human cells.

specific virus type, the virus either enters the host cell in its entirety or injects its nucleic acid into the host, takes command, and reproduces.

Certain RNA viruses—called retroviruses—contain an enzyme called reverse transcriptase. This enzyme allows virus RNA to make a DNA copy of itself inside the host. This becomes a permanent part of the host's genome. The virus that causes AIDS is an example of a retrovirus.

BACTERIOPHAGES

It may be hard to imagine bacteria being "sick" but actually, they are at risk of infection by viruses called bacteriophages. The name *bacteriophage* means "bacteria eater"; this gives an idea of how deadly these infections are. When a bacteriophage lands on a suitable bacterial cell, the virus injects its DNA into the host cell. The host cell's biochemical machinery converts to a virus making "factory." Once enough bacteriophages are made, the bacterial cell bursts open, dying and releasing a population of new viruses ready to infect other bacteria.

Interestingly, medical researchers are turning to bacteriophages to help us fight human disease. Because so many bacteria are becoming resistant to the antibiotics used to control infection, scientists are studying phage therapy, the use of bacteriophages to combat bacterial infections in humans.

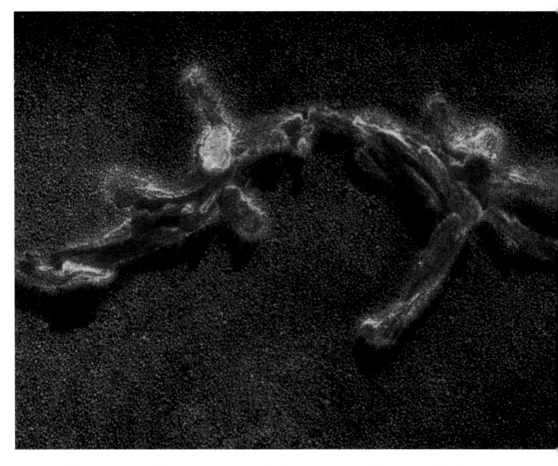

This scanning electron micrograph shows prions taken from the brain of a hamster infected with scrapie.

How Do Prions Work?

Like viruses, prions—infectious proteins—are not alive; however, unlike viruses, prions contain no genetic material. Prion-like particles are found in the brain and have a normal function there, perhaps involving the storage of very long-term memories. When these normal proteins change their shapes to an abnormal form, they become pathogenic by forcing other prion-like particles to misfold into abnormal forms. The transformation from normal to "bad" spreads and the prions make clumps inside the brain, damaging delicate cell structures. Prions produce degenerative diseases of the nervous system such mad cow disease, scrapie (in sheep), and Creutzfeldt-Jakob disease (in humans). Animals or persons afflicted with these diseases lose control of their nervous systems and brain functions. These diseases are extremely rare, which is fortunate because prions are virtually indestructible, and the diseases they cause untreatable at present. Prions are the only pathogens that are invisible to the immune system.

Bibliography

Alberts, Bruce, Dennis Bray, Karen Hopkin, Alexander D. Johnson, Julian Lewis, Martin Raff, Keith Roberts, and Peter Walter. *Essential Cell Biology*, 4th edition. New York, NY: Garland Science, 2013.

Bonner, John Tyler. *The Evolution of Complexity by Means of Natural Selection*. Princeton, NJ: Princeton University Press, 1988.

Bonner, John Tyler. *The Social Amoebae: The Biology of Cellular Slime Molds*. Princeton, NJ: Princeton University Press, 2009.

Bozzone, Donna M., and Douglas S. Green. *Biology for the Informed Citizen*. New York, NY: Oxford University Press, 2013.

Crick, Francis. *What Mad Pursuit: A Personal View of Scientific Discovery*. New York, NY: Basic Books, 1990.

Geison, Gerald L. *The Private Science of Louis Pasteur*. Princeton, NJ: Princeton University Press, 1995.

Harris, Henry. *The Birth of the Cell*. New Haven, CT: Yale University Press, 2000.

Jardine, Lisa. *The Curious Life of Robert Hooke: The Man Who Measured London*. New York, NY: Harper Collins Publishers, 2004.

Kennedy, Michael T. *A Brief History of Disease, Science and Medicine*. Mission Viejo, CA: Asklepiad Press, 2004.

Lagerkvsit, Ulf. *Pioneers of Microbiology and the Nobel Prize.* London, England: World Scientific, 2003.

Maddox, Brenda. *Rosalind Franklin: The Dark Lady of DNA.* New York, NY: Harper Collins Publishers, 2002.

Magner, Lois N. *History of the Life Sciences*, 3rd edition. New York, NY: CRC Press, 2002.

Magner, Lois N. *A History of Medicine*, 2nd edition. New York, NY: CRC Press, 2005.

Moore, John A. *Science as a Way of Knowing: The Foundations of Modern Biology.* Cambridge, MA: Harvard University Press, 1993.

Tortora, Gerard J., Berdell R. Funke , and Christine L. Case. *Microbiology: An Introduction*, 12th edition. New York, NY: Pearson, 2016.

Glossary

aerobic Living in the presence of oxygen.

amino acid One of several building blocks of proteins.

anaerobic Living in the absence of oxygen.

antiseptic A substance that kills bacteria and other microbes.

binary fission A type of cell division in prokaryotes that produces identical cells.

biomass The weight of organisms.

chemoautotroph An organism that extracts energy from hydrogen, hydrogen sulfide, or iron and uses carbon dioxide as a carbon source.

chemoheterotroph An organism that uses molecules such as sugar as a source of energy and carbon.

chromosome The structure on which genes are located.

cilia Structures that are similar to eukaryotic flagella but more numerous and shorter, which help cells swim.

codon A set of three nucleotides that designates a specific amino acid to be used in protein production.

conjugation The process in which prokaryotic cells connect to each other by a tube and exchange DNA.

cytoplasm The gel-like material in cells.

cytoskeleton The fibers and motor proteins in eukaryotic cells that are needed for cell movement.

decomposition The breakdown of waste materials.

electron microscopy A technique that focuses a beam of electrons to magnify objects for observation.

enzyme A protein that controls chemical reactions in cells.

eukaryote A cell that has a nucleus and organelles.

flagellum In prokaryotes, a propeller-like structure that spins to move cells; in eukaryotes, a whip-like structure that bends vigorously to move cells.

gamete A sex cell; an egg or sperm in humans.

gene The basic unit of heredity; genes have the instruction for making proteins.

genetics The study of heredity.

genome The entire set of genes in an organism.

light microscopy A technique that uses lenses to focus light in order to magnify objects for observation.

meiosis The type of cell division in eukaryotes that produces gametes.

methanogen A microbe that produces methane.

miasma A bad odor once thought to cause disease.

mitosis The type of cell division in eukaryotes that produces identical cells.

motile Able to move or locomote.

mutation An alteration in the sequence of nucleotides in a gene.

myxamoeba A type of amoeba found in cellular slime molds.

nitrogen cycling The movement of nitrogen through the environment.

nitrogen fixation The process of converting nitrogen gas into nitrogen-containing molecules that organisms can use.

nucleotide One of several building blocks of DNA and RNA.

nucleus The structure in a eukaryotic cell where chromosomes are located.

organelle A specialized structure in eukaryotic cells; each organelle performs specific functions.

pasteurization A technique to heat foods and beverages to prevent bacterial growth.

photoautotroph An organism that uses sunlight as an energy source and carbon dioxide as a carbon source.

photoheterotroph An organism that uses sunlight as an energy source and molecules such as sugars as a carbon source.

photosynthesis The process of using the energy of the sun to convert carbon dioxide into sugar.

plasmodium A giant cell of plasmodial slime molds; the feeding stage.

prion An infectious protein.

prokaryote A type of microbe that lacks a nucleus or organelles.

pseudopod A blob-like extension of an amoeba that permits crawling locomotion.

ribosomes Structures that assemble amino acids into proteins.

RNA polymerase An enzyme that makes RNA.

spore The resting stage formed by some microbes when environmental conditions become poor.

symbiosis A close relationship between two organisms where both benefit.

taxonomist An expert in the classification of organisms.

transduction The movement of a piece of DNA from one cell to another using a virus as a carrier.

transformation The capacity of cells to take up DNA freely present in their environment.

zygote A single cell produced when gametes fuse together.

Further Reading

Books

Favor, Lesli J. *Bacteria.* New York, NY: Rosen Central, 2017.

Hirsch, Rebecca E. *The Human Microbiome: The Germs That Keep You Healthy.* Minneapolis, MN: Twenty-First Century Books, 2017.

Landon, Melissa. *Biology: Understanding Living Matter.* New York: NY: Rosen Publishing Group, 2015.

Merchant, Raina G., and Lesli J. Favor. *How Eukaryotic and Prokaryotic Cells Differ.* New York, NY: Rosen Publishing Group, 2015.

Randolph, Joanne. *Microbes: The Good, the Bad, and the Ugly.* New York, NY: Enslow Publishing, 2018.

Sherman, Irwin W. *The Power of Plagues.* Washington, DC: ASM Press, 2017.

Smith, Linda Wasmer. *Louis Pasteur: Genius Disease Fighter.* Berkley Heights, NJ: Enslow Publishers, 2015.

Websites

American Society for Microbiology

www.asm.org

The society's mission is to advance microbiology as a way to understand life processes and to apply and communicate this knowledge worldwide for the improvement of health and for environmental and economic well-being.

Centers for Disease Control and Prevention

www.cdc.gov/genomics/

The Office of Public Health Genomics was founded in 1997 to help incorporate genomics into public health research, policy, and programs.

Genetics Society of America (GSA)

www.genetics-gsa.org

The GSA works to improve communication between geneticists, promote research, foster the training of the next generation of geneticists, and educate the public and government about advances in genetics and their consequences to individuals and society.

Microscopy Society of America (MSA)

www.microscopy.org

Founded in 1942, the MSA is dedicated to the promotion and advancement of techniques and applications of microscopy and microanalysis in all relevant fields of science.

Index

friction, 36, 38, 61
fruit flies, 25
fungi, 5

G

gametes, 25
genes, 22–25, 28–29, 33, 40, 55, 61, 63
genetics, 22–23, 25
genome, 22, 51, 69
germ theory, 13, 15, 17
green algae, 18, 61–63

H

heredity, 22–23
Hooke, Robert, 11, 13, 18
hosts, 51, 55, 67, 69
human body, 9, 52, 59
Human Microbiome Project, 9

I

inheritance, 22–23, 25, 28, 33

K

Koch, Robert, 15, 17, 19–20

L

Leeuwenhoek, Anton van, 11, 13, 18
light microscopy, 13
Lister, Joseph, 15, 20

M

MacLoed, Colin, 28
macrocysts, 66
macrophages, 59
McCarty, Maclyn, 28
miasmas, 13, 15
meiosis, 25, 27
microbes,
    decomposition, 41, 43
    disease, 13–17
    in food, 7, 17, 21
Micrographia, 18
microscopes, 11, 13, 17, 18
Mendel, Gregor, 23–25
methane, 48
Miescher, Friedrich, 28
mitochondria, 51, 54–55
mitosis, 59, 61, 63–64
molecular biology, 28
Morgan, T. H., 25, 28
mutation, 33, 40

N

National Institutes of Health (NIH), 9
Nirenberg, Marshall, 29
nitrogen cycle, 41, 43
nitrogen fixation, 41
Nobel Prize, 31
nucleotides, 29
nucleus, 51